Everything the Internet
didn't teach you about
Crochet

by Jean Leinhauser and Rita Weiss

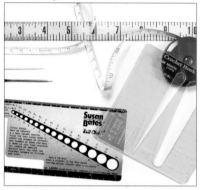

complete tool guide

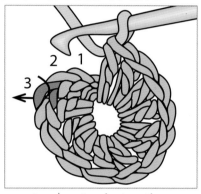

step-by-step instructions

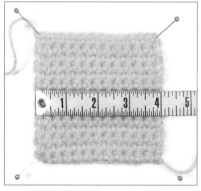

learning about gauge

plus easy beginner projects

Leisure Arts, Inc.
Maumelle, Arkansas

Produced by

Production Team

Creative Directors: Jean Leinhauser and Rita Weiss

Senior Editor: Susan Lowman

Photographer: Carol Wilson Mansfield

Book Design: Linda Causee

Diagrams © 2013 by The Creative Partners™LLC

Reproduced by special permission

Library of Congress Control Number: 2012955764

ISBN-13: 978-1-4647-0741-4

Introduction

The original plan for this book was an idea conceived by my co-author Jean Leinhauser. Jean has always been well known as a supporter of crochet with the many books she has written over the 50 years of her career. Most of all, however, Jean was a teacher. She loved teaching crochet, stimulating newbies to pursue a rich life stitching.

I have watched her teach in the strangest places. My favorite was finding her recuperating in a hospital bed with an entire room of hospital personnel holding crochet hooks and carefully following her instructions.

The fact that more and more people were teaching themselves to crochet by following presentations on the Internet fascinated her. On the one hand, it delighted her to know that new crocheters were being hatched. However, it concerned her that by teaching themselves to crochet, new crocheters were missing a lot. They may have learned the basic stitches, but they haven't learned about the various types of crochet hooks. No one has taught them how to evaluate yarns and to distinguish one from the other. They've never learned about the importance of gauge and how to make a gauge swatch. They would not know how to read a crochet pattern or to decipher the meaning of symbols, asterisks, daggers and brackets.

So Jean decided to produce this book for all those crocheters out there who learned from the Internet.

Unfortunately, Jean died before we could finish this book. We were most fortunate, however, in being able to work with Jean's friend, Susan Lowman, who stepped up and helped to finish the book. In addition to working as the technical editor on the book, Susan designed the three projects that Jean wanted to include.

At Jean's suggestion, we have added our Refresher Course in Crochet. If you can't remember what the Internet taught you, or if you're just not crocheting with the ease that other crocheters around you seem to have, then turn to page 71 for Jean's instructions. But if you just need some help in reading a yarn label or in determining whether a pattern could possibly be too difficult for you, you've come to the right place.

Here are the answers to those questions you could find no one to ask.

– Rita Weiss

Contents

Tools 5

Yarn 19

The Importance of Gauge 37

Reading a Pattern.. 41

Working a Pattern 47

Making Fringe and Tassels................................. 67

Refresher Course in Crochet.............................. 71

Index 96

Tools

One of the great advantages of deciding you want to be a crocheter is the realization that you won't need a lot of tools. If you wanted to make furniture instead of just crocheting afghans and sweaters, you'd need a lot of saws, hammers, nails, awls, screwdrivers and more. To be a crocheter, all you really need is the proper crochet hook and some yarn.

Crochet Hooks

There are basically two types of crochet hooks used today: those to be used for yarn and those to be used with thinner threads for fine, lace weight projects. While there are other types of hooks such as double-ended or circular hooks with a hook at one or both ends, these two are the most common.

Yarn Hook

Thread (steel) Hook

Yarn Crochet Hooks

Crochet hooks for use with yarn are made in a variety of materials, each of which has advantages or disadvantages, but most of them have the same basic construction.

(A) Head: This is the business end of the hook, which will slide in and out of the work as needed, and which will grab or hook the yarn so you can draw it through easily. Different hook brands may have different-shaped heads, but all are used in the same way.

(B) Throat: The slanted part that goes from the head to the working area. Do not work on the throat or your stitches will be much too tight.

(C) Working area: This is the most important part of the hook. Here, on this straight area, the stitches are formed and "set" into their final size. Make certain that all stitches are worked well up on this area.

(D) Finger hold: An indented space where you can place your thumb to help balance the work. Never use this space to form the stitches, or they will be much too loose. Not all hooks have the finger hold. Which type you prefer is up to you; they both work equally well. It is a matter of personal preference.

(E) Shaft: This is where the hand rests as you work.

Yarn Crochet Hook Materials

Crochet hooks for yarn crocheting are made in a variety of materials, each of which has advantages and disadvantages. The three main materials used today for hooks for crocheting with yarn are: plastic, metal (such as aluminum), and wood (including bamboo). Years ago crochet hooks were made of other materials like bone, especially whale bone. These hooks are no longer sold today and have become collector's items. Today's crocheter can choose the hook that fits her particular style and the project that she is working on. The kind of hook to be used is an individual choice made by the crocheter. Often the choice depends upon the stitches being used and the type of yarn as well as the crocheter's own special crocheting habits.

Plastic hooks are probably the most common crochet hooks used and tend to be cool to the touch. They allow the yarn to slip well through stitches, but can be uncomfortable when used for long periods of time. Purchasing a rubber handle, which fits over the shaft of the crochet hook, can make it more comfortable for use.

Metal hooks (including aluminum, steel, nickel-plated): While steel hooks are mainly used in thread work, some yarn hooks are made of metal as well. These tend to be cool to the touch and are great for crocheters who want to work fast, as there is very little friction. They very rarely will bend or break, so they will last a long time. Some crocheters, however, find them too slippery. Some crocheters feel that metal hooks work best when working with yarns that might stick to the hook such as wools, alpaca or angora yarns. If, however, the yarn is a slippery one, such as silks or rayons, metal hooks are probably not a good choice. Aluminum hooks are best if the crocheter is looking for a light metal hook, or if she wishes to neutralize warm hands. Aluminum hooks are readily available in most craft stores and tend to be fairly inexpensive. Their smooth surface allows the stitches to move very quickly and with very little resistance. Since many metal hooks are nickel-plated, the crocheter needs to be aware of any allergies to nickel. Metal tends to be unyielding, and this may prove a problem for those with arthritis, carpal tunnel syndrome or sensitive hands.

Wood hooks (including bamboo): While bamboo is actually not a wood, it has all of the properties of wood and is therefore classified with wood hooks. These hooks are often slightly longer than metal or plastic hooks. Wood hooks can be made of birch, ebony, rosewood, or walnut, and they often have detailed, carved handles. These hooks are usually treated with a coating to keep them from wearing out. This means that the process moves more slowly and precisely, but that is an advantage when working with complex patterns or when starting to learn to crochet. These hooks are warmer, more flexible and lighter in weight than most aluminum hooks. The disadvantage of wooden hooks is their tendency to break or splinter; in addition, hooks made of rarer woods can be expensive.

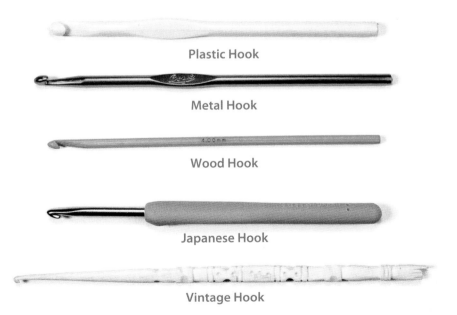

Plastic Hook

Metal Hook

Wood Hook

Japanese Hook

Vintage Hook

These hooks are a great choice for beginners as they tend to grab the yarn as you work. Experienced crocheters are often turned off by wood's ability to grip the yarn as this can slow down the work. Smaller sizes break easily, and larger sizes are heavy and add to the weight of the project.

Japanese hooks are probably the most comfortable hooks to use. They have a wide, cushioned handle, which makes them very comfortable, especially for crocheters who use the knife hold (see page 72). Japanese hooks come in sets or can be purchased individually. They are often more expensive than aluminum, plastic and steel hooks, but are especially valuable for crocheters who do a lot of crocheting.

Vintage hooks were made years ago from ivory, bone, early plastics, metals and wood. Many of these hooks had handles made from Mother of Pearl, agate, cork, Sterling silver or were gold plated. These hooks are no longer sold today and have become collector's items. The ones that are in good condition (smooth and clean) can still be used today. If they are not marked with a size, use a hook size gauge to determine the size.

The choice of type of material chosen for your hook is strictly up to the individual crocheter. Choose the hook that works best for you and for the project that you are making. No one can tell you what type of hook you want. Once you have become proficient at crocheting, you might want to invest in some of the exotic hooks currently on the market. Many of these hooks are hand crafted from magnificent woods, such as rosewood, birch or ebony. Many of these hooks are quite expensive, so wait until you are certain that you want that particular size hook before you make your purchase.

Crochet hooks come in a variety of diameters and lengths and in two basic types, inline and shaped.

Inline   Shaped

Hook Diameter

The diameter of the crochet hook determines the size of the hook. For a long time there was a great deal of confusion on the numbers listed for sizes on crochet hooks.

Different manufacturers often used different markings. Some used a system of letters and some used a number system. In addition, there were two different methods used to size hooks in the US, in the UK, and Canada. Some hook manufacturers even included a metric equivalent. Several years ago the Craft Yarn Council, an organization of yarn manufacturers, yarn publishers and hook and needle manufacturers, agreed to make metric (millimeter/mm) sizing more prominent on packaging and to list the US sizes, both numbers and/or letters, on the packaging.

In the metric system, a lower number indicates a thinner yarn hook. In the US, the same rule applies to sizes of hooks: lower numbers indicate thinner hooks. Unfortunately in the UK, the sizing is the exact opposite: lower numbers indicate thicker hooks. The chart on page 13 shows hook sizes in both the US and the UK. Interestingly, the only time when the hook sizes match is on the size 7 (4.5 mm). If you still have a question about hook size, use a hook gauge (see page 16). Hooks above 10mm (US Size 15) are usually called "Jiffy Hooks" because the large diameter makes the work move very quickly and usually produces a very loosely woven fabric.

Yarn Hook Conversion Chart

Metric	US	UK/Canadian
2.0 mm	-	14
2.25 mm	B/1	13
2.5 mm	-	12
2.75 mm	C/2	-
3.0 mm	-	11
3.25 mm	D/3	10
3.5 mm	E/4	9
3.75 mm	F/5	-
4.0 mm	G/6	8
4.5 mm	7	7
5.0 mm	H/8	6
5.5 mm	I/9	5
6.0 mm	J/10	4
6.5 mm	K/$10^1/_2$	3
7.0 mm	-	2
8.0 mm	L/11	0
9.0 mm	M,N/13	00
10.0 mm	N,P/15	000

Thread Crochet Hooks

Thread crochet hooks are tiny hooks that are used to make very fine, lace weight projects, such as doilies and tablecloths. They are designed to be used with thinner threads than regular yarn crochet. These hooks are about 5" long, which is shorter than most hooks used for yarns, and are constructed slightly differently. These hooks are made from steel because it is a harder metal than aluminum and is less liable to break at the hook end, which is very narrow on the smallest steel hooks. Some steel hooks come with a plastic handle or you can purchase a rubber handle to place over your steel hook to make the grip more comfortable, especially when crocheting for long periods of time.

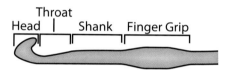

The hook end is a little sharper than found on yarn hooks; then comes the throat, which gradually becomes thicker until it forms the shank, the area on which the stitches must be formed. Then the hook thickens again until it reaches the finger grip. It is important that every stitch be made on the shank, not on the throat (which will cause the stitches to be too tight) or on the area beyond the shank (which will cause the stitches to be too loose).

Steel thread crochet hooks are sized differently from regular yarn hooks. In fact the sizing is the exact opposite. The higher the number, the smaller the hook, which is the reverse of yarn hook sizing. Steel thread crochet hooks sold by American manufacturers range in size from 14 (the finest) to 00 (the thickest). Even finer hooks are sold in other countries where much more delicate lace work is created.

Different countries use different numbering systems, and this chart can help clear up any confusion. It shows hook sizes in both the US and the UK. If you still have a question about steel hook size, use a gauge (see page 16).

Steel Hook Conversion Chart

Metric	US	UK/Canadian
3.5 mm	00	—
3.25 mm	0	0
2.75 mm	1	1
2.25 mm	2	$1^1/_2$
2.1 mm	3	2
2.0 mm	4	$2^1/_2$
1.9 mm	5	3
1.8 mm	6	$3^1/_2$
1.65 mm	7	4
1.5 mm	8	$4^1/_2$
1.4 mm	9	5
1.3 mm	10	$5^1/_2$
1.1 mm	11	6
1.0 mm	12	$6^1/_2$
.85 mm	13	7
.75 mm	14	—

Other Crochet Tools

While all of these tools are not necessary for everyday crocheting, it is handy to have at least some of them.

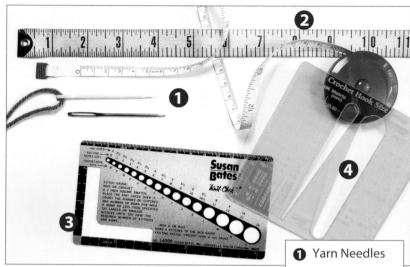

1 Yarn Needles
2 Tape Measure
3 Hook Gauge
4 Tapered slot hook gauge

Needle/Hook Gauge: This is a valuable instrument for checking the correct size of any hook even if the size is actually stamped on the hook. Some crochet hooks are not marked so once they are removed from their wrappers, the only way you can determine size is to use a needle/hook gauge. These sizers are made from a flat piece of plastic or metal with holes of various sizes or tapered slots that correspond to hook sizes. Many crocheters prefer the gauge with a tapered slot because they feel that this type of gauge shows the true physical size of a hook. For more information on gauge, see pages 37-40.

Small Scissors: Use these to cut the yarn when necessary. Never tear the yarn as this could stretch the fibers.

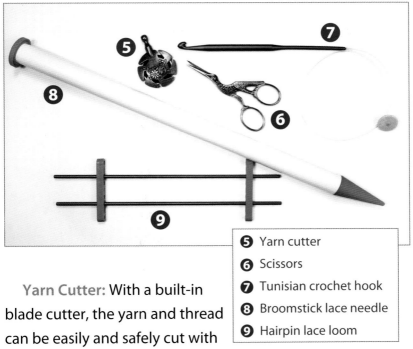

5 Yarn cutter
6 Scissors
7 Tunisian crochet hook
8 Broomstick lace needle
9 Hairpin lace loom

Yarn Cutter: With a built-in blade cutter, the yarn and thread can be easily and safely cut with any of the grooves. For crocheters who travel by airplane, this is a most valuable replacement for scissors, which are sometimes confiscated.

Yarn Needle: A needle with a large eye and a blunt end that is used to sew pieces together and to weave in ends.

Tape Measure: Use this to check your gauge and to measure your crochet. It is a good idea to have one that reads in both centimeters and inches.

As you learn more about crochet, you may want to include these tools for making broomstick lace, hairpin lace or Tunisian crochet.

Broomstick Lace Needle: A long, wide needle used to make Broomstick Lace (aka: Jiffy Lace). This plastic needle comes in various diameters, such as 25 mm, 19 mm and 10 mm and is used to create fast, open, lacy crochet fabric.

Hairpin Lace Loom: A tool for making Hairpin Lace, a crochet technique which creates a lacy crochet fabric. Many hairpin lace looms have adjustable widths from 1" to 4" wide.

Tunisian Crochet Hook: Longer than a regular hook to hold a large number of stitches, the Tunisian crochet hook often has a knob on one end like a knitting needle or—as pictured on page 17—a cable for accommodating a wide strip of crochet. Most of these hooks are smooth from end to end without a finger hold in the middle. It is also known as the Afghan stitch hook.

Yarn

One of the most confusing things for new crocheters is to choose a yarn from the vast choices that there are today. Which is the yarn that will work up quickly? Which is the yarn that will look lovely as a warm sweater? Which is the yarn to use for making a baby's blanket?

Several years ago the members of the Craft Yarn Council joined together to try to set up some guidelines for the marketplace. To help consumers select the right materials for a project, they set up the following standard yarn weight system because even different fibers have a common denominator: weight.

Weight

Yarn is classified by weight, which really refers to its thickness. Yarns can be so very thin that they are used to make lace, or as fat as your little finger.

Here are the seven categories and the logos used to indicate each category.

Lace, 10 count crochet thread, Fingering. Lace weight yarns and threads are used to create openwork patterns for such projects as doilies, tablecloths and bedspreads. They are usually worked on steel crochet hooks which are sized differently from yarn hooks; the higher the number, the smaller the hook. Lace weight threads and yarns are often crocheted on larger hooks to create the openwork pattern. A gauge range, therefore, is difficult to determine. Always follow the gauge indicated in the pattern.

Sock, Fingering, Baby Yarn.

This is the yarn most often used for baby items and socks. There are 5.25 to 8 stitches per inch on sizes B/1 to E/4 (2.25mm to 3.5mm) crochet hooks.

Sport, Baby Yarn.

("Sport" has nothing to do with athletic events; it is used rather as in women's sportswear.) This yarn is thicker than baby weight yarn, and works for socks, shawls, wraps and accessories. There are 4 to 5 stitches per inch on sizes E/4 to 7 (3.5mm to 4.5 mm) crochet hooks.

DK, Light Worsted Weight Yarn.

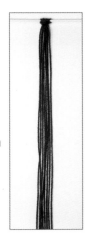

This yarn is just a bit thicker than sport weight and is slightly lighter than the medium weight yarn. There are 3 to 4.25 stitches per inch on sizes 7 to I/9 (4.5 mm to 5.5 mm) crochet hooks. The name derives from Worstead, a village in the English county of Norfolk. This village, together with North Walsham and Aylsham, became a manufacturing center for yarn and cloth after weavers from Flanders immigrated to Norfolk in the 12th century.

MEDIUM 4 Worsted, Afghan, Aran yarns.

The most popular and most commonly used yarn, this is only slightly heavier than the yarn in the Number 3 category. It is used for afghans, sweaters, hats, scarves, gloves and almost anything else a crocheter might want to make. There are 2.75 to 3.5 stitches per inch on sizes I/9 to K/10 1/2 (5.5 mm to 6.5 mm) crochet hooks.

Tip: 4-ply yarn is a term often used mistakenly to refer to worsted weight yarn. All yarn is made up of a number of plies, or strands, that are twisted together to make the strand you will work with. Baby weight yarn can be made of four plies, and worsted weight yarn can be made of just two plies; it all depends upon the thickness of each ply. So just because a yarn is made of four plies does not mean it is worsted weight.

BULKY
5 Chunky, Craft, Rug. These yarns are about twice as thick as the worsted weight yarns. Use large hooks, and this yarn can work up very, very quickly. It is used for throws, felted items and heavy sweaters. There are 2 to 2.75 stitches per inch on sizes K/10^1/$_2$ to M/13 (6.5 mm to 9 mm) crochet hooks.

SUPER BULKY
6 Bulky, Roving. These yarns are the "absolute" for creating crochet projects in a hurry. A project made with these yarns could be completed in a few hours or at the most a few days. There are 1.25 to 2.25 stitches per inch on sizes M/13 and larger (9 mm and larger) crochet hooks.

For the complete Craft Yarn Council chart for the Standard Yarn Weight System which lists the categories and gives recommended hooks, see page 96.

The weight of the yarn you use has a great deal to do with what the finished project will look like. On the next page, there are seven swatches, each made with a different weight of yarn and the suggested hook size. Each swatch has the same number of stitches and the same number of rows.

SUPER BULKY 6 **Lion Brand® Yarn Quick & Cozy**
Size N-13 (9 mm) hook

BULKY 5 **Caron® Dazzleaire**
Size K-10 1/2 (6.5 mm) hook

MEDIUM 4 **Red Heart® Super Saver®**
Size I-9 (5.5 mm) hook

LIGHT 3 **Patons® Astra**
Size G-6 (4 mm) hook

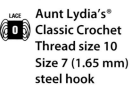

FINE 2 **Lion Brand®
Yarn Vanna's
Glamour®**
Size E-4
(3.5 mm) hook

SUPER FINE 1 **Red Heart®
Stardust™**
Size B-1
(2.25 mm) hook

LACE 0 **Aunt Lydia's®
Classic Crochet
Thread size 10**
Size 7 (1.65 mm)
steel hook

Fibers

Many different types of fiber are used in yarn for crochet. Your choice of fiber is important in selecting the best product to be used in a project. Different fibers require different care in the completed project as well as determine the drape and feel of the finished work. Certain yarns are more suitable for certain uses. If you are making something for a baby or child that will require frequent washing, choose a yarn that is strong and machine washable. To be perfectly safe, trust your pattern and follow the instructions for fiber choice until you know how various fibers will wear.

Here is a description of some of the most popular yarns for crocheting.

Acrylic

Acrylics are one of the most common fibers used today. This is a synthetic fiber made from acrylonitrile, which comes from coal, air, water, petroleum and limestone. The yarn, which is very resilient and moderately strong, has a good resistance to sunlight and will last through many launderings.

Angora

The yarn comes from the Angora rabbit and is gently harvested during the rabbit's natural molting process. Eight times warmer than sheep wool, it is so light that it provides warmth without weight. The fiber lacks elasticity so it is sometimes blended with sheep wool to give the yarn a bit of stretch.

Bamboo

Bamboo is a grass that can be spun into a fiber. Since it can be harvested without killing the plant, and it only takes a few months before it is ready to be harvested again, it is an environmentally friendly choice. The yarn is cool and silky, soft to the touch and works up beautifully in anything where a drape is desired.

Cashmere

One of the most exotic and rarest fibers, cashmere is the soft undercoat of the Kashmir goat. It is a soft, lightweight and warm yarn that maintains its softness in a variety of weights. It is such a delicate yarn that it is often blended with wool to make it more durable. Because the goat only produces a few ounces of yarn each year, cashmere remains one of the most expensive of fibers.

Cotton

Cotton is a soft, staple fiber that grows around the seeds of the cotton plant. Although the yarn is non-allergenic, moisture absorbing and very strong, it is heavy and dense and contains a limited amount of elasticity. It actually is weaker than silk or linen but stronger than wool. Mercerized cotton, which is produced by adding caustic acid to the cotton, is stronger and is produced in a variety of beautiful colors.

Linen

Linen, which is made from the fibers of the flax plant, is naturally crisp, strong and lustrous. It is not soft, which discourages many crocheters. However, when it is blended with other fibers such as wool, it retains its silkiness. It is durable, stronger than any other fiber and absorbs moisture.

Microfibers

This is the name for synthetic fibers that measure less than one denier. The most common types are made from polyester or nylon or a combination of the two. Because the fibers are so fine, the properties of the regular sized fibers are changed. The spun yarns have more drape and a very soft feel, but they do not lose their yarn structure. Garments made with microfibers do not sag or droop. Microfiber yarns feel more like natural fibers than regular synthetic yarns. The yarn is much more heat sensitive, however, and a project made with microfibers should never be touched with an iron nor placed in a clothes dryer.

Mohair

Mohair comes from the coat of the Angora goat, and is both durable and resilient. Known for its high luster and sheen, it is often used in fiber blends to add these qualities to other yarns. The yarn is also warm and like wool has great insulating properties. Mohair is soft and fuzzy, but it can be very irritating to the skin. Therefore, mohair sweaters are often lined with silk or cotton, or the mohair yarn is mixed with other fibers for comfort.

Nylon

Nylon is the generic name for a whole group of synthetic polymers known as polyamides. Nylon was the first synthetic fiber to be made entirely from coal, water and air. Nylon is lightweight but strong and very washable. It is elastic, but does not stretch or shrink unless it is subjected to very high temperatures. Nylon is often combined with wool to give wool strength and elasticity especially in sock yarns.

Polyester

Polyester is another synthetic fiber which is strong and resistant to stretching and shrinking while remaining very washable. It is often combined with other fibers to add strength and resilience. Combined with cotton, it makes the cotton more absorbent while a combination of polyester and wool helps the wool maintain its shape in all types of weather. When it is added to rayon and nylon, the resulting yarns have better drape and are strong, durable and easy to launder.

Rayon

Rayon is not a natural fiber, but it is made from naturally occurring ingredients that have required extensive processing before the threads are created. It is actually the oldest manufactured fiber, having been in production since the 1880s. Rayon is highly absorbent, can be hand washed and dries quickly. It drapes well and is so easy to dye that rayon is available in a variety of colors. The thread is frequently blended with other fibers and often is used instead of silk. The yarn is slippery, however, and requires a bit of skill in working with it.

Silk

Although silk is not strictly an animal fiber, it does have some of the same properties because it has a protein structure. It doesn't conduct heat so silk is an excellent insulator and will serve to keep the recipient of a silk garment cool in the summer and warm in the winter. Silk yarn will create a light, velvety-soft ultrasmooth garment that will not shrink or stretch.

Soy

Creating yarn from vegetable fibers, like soy, is not new; actually cotton and linen are made from vegetable fibers. Recently with the new interest from environmentalists in the development of eco-friendly products, new soy yarns have arrived on the market. Although there are yarns made of 100% soy, most soy yarns are blended with wool or acrylic. These yarns have a beautiful sheen and drape beautifully.

Wool

While the term "wool" is used often to mean any fiber shorn from an animal, to crocheters the term "wool" refers to the fiber that comes from sheep. This is probably the most durable and versatile of all fibers used in crocheting. A wool garment retains its shape and resists wrinkles so it is able to absorb perspiration, releasing it gradually thereby making a wool garment comfortable year around. Wool is easily dyed and flame retardant. Wool should be washed and dried by hand; however, if washed in very hot water and dried in a dryer, the wool will felt. This may be desirable since "felting" is a technique that produces interesting results. Superwashed wool has been treated to prevent felting and can be washed in a washer.

Merino Wool was originally a term used to describe wool from merino sheep in Spain. This was the finest and softest wool. Today merino wool comes from other places, and the term is used to describe the very best soft wool.

Choosing Your Yarn: The Ball Band

When you go to buy yarn, you will find yourself surrounded by all kinds of yarns in different fibers, in various weights besides being in the color you want. If you can find a knowledgeable sales assistant to help you, you're in luck. If, however, you are alone, don't despair. Every yarn in the store can help you because every yarn in the store is enclosed with a ball band that tells you everything you need to know about that particular yarn. Once you have learned to read a ball band, you'll never be afraid to buy yarn again.

Yarn is packaged differently by different manufacturers and by the type of yarn. Sometimes it is sold as a hank, which is a coil of loosely wound yarn. That type of yarn will require your winding it into a ball before you begin to crochet. Some yarn is pre-wound into a ball or skein, and the ball band will often give you information on how to pull the yarn onto your hook. Almost all yarn, however it is packaged, will have a ball band with the important information.

While a salesperson in a store can help you with this information, if you learn to read a ball band, you will always be able to learn everything about a yarn.

The ball band label will tell you all you need to know to make an intelligent choice of yarn. It will give you the name of the manufacturer and the manufacturer's web address, the name of the yarn and its fiber content, the amount of yarn in the ball and where the yarn was made.

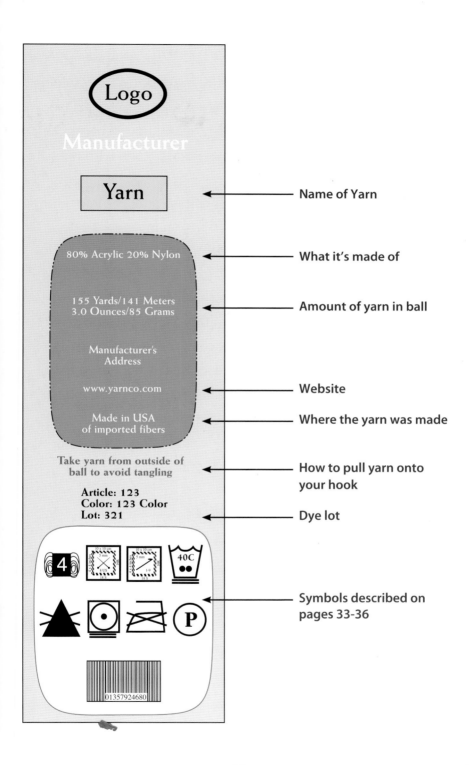

Logo

Manufacturer

Yarn ← Name of Yarn

80% Acrylic 20% Nylon ← What it's made of

155 Yards/141 Meters
3.0 Ounces/85 Grams ← Amount of yarn in ball

Manufacturer's
Address

www.yarnco.com ← Website

Made in USA
of imported fibers ← Where the yarn was made

Take yarn from outside of
ball to avoid tangling ← How to pull yarn onto
your hook

Article: 123
Color: 123 Color
Lot: 321 ← Dye lot

← Symbols described on
pages 33-36

The label will give you the yarn weight category symbol that was discussed on pages 20 - 23 along with a chart showing what size of hook will work best to attain the necessary gauge, which shows how many stitches and rows it will take to make a 4" swatch. (See pages 37-40 for a further explanation of gauge.) It will also tell you how to take care of a project made with the yarn.

The label will also give you the specific color of the yarn along with the dye lot. It is very important that you make certain that all of the yarn for a specific project comes from the same dye lot. Yarns that have dye lots listed are dyed in batches, somewhere about 3,000 skeins at a time. Because each batch is dyed individually, and factors such as humidity, water pH, and others can have an effect on the dyeing process, the yarn is given a dye lot number. Some yarns have no dye lot because they are made from colored fiber purchased from a fiber supplier. The color is injected as the fiber is formed, and it becomes an intrinsic part of the fiber itself. So long as the fiber is made the same way and provided by the same supplier, the color remains consistent.

The final part of the label gives you symbols which tell you about the yarn you are using. The first symbol shows you the size or weight of the yarn as discussed on pages 20 - 23.

The next symbol suggests the size of hook you should use and the gauge that you should attain using this hook (See pages 37 - 40 for an explanation of gauge).

The "H-8" and the "5 mm" indicate that the average crocheter should use a size H-8 (5 mm) crochet hook to work with this yarn. The label now tells you that with your size H-8 hook, you should make a 4" x 4" (10 x 10 cm) square in which you will probably achieve 16 rows and each row will be 12 single crochet stitches. That says that with this yarn, you will get about 3 stitches to an inch ($12 \div 4 = 3$), and 4 rows to an inch ($16 \div 4 = 4$). Crocheters should always make their own gauge swatch using the suggested gauge as a jumping-off point!

The same information is given in the other square for knitting.

In the last part of the label, there is a list of laundering and dry cleaning symbols. Here are some of the most popular symbols.

Note: System of dots indicating temperature range is the same for all wash procedures.

Symbol   Meaning

 Machine Wash, Normal: Garment made from this yarn may be laundered through use of a machine designed for this purpose.

 Machine Wash, Cold: Initial water temperature should not exceed 30° centigrade or 86° Fahrenheit.

 Machine Wash, Warm: Initial water temperature should not exceed 40° centigrade or 104° Fahrenheit.

 Machine Wash, Gentle or Delicate: Garment made from this yarn may be machine laundered only on the setting designed for gentle agitation and/or reduced time for delicate items.

 Hand Wash: Garment made from this yarn may be laundered through use of water, detergent or soap and gentle hand manipulation. Required water temperature is indicated by the number of dots.

Symbol	Meaning

 Do Not Wash: Garment made from this yarn may not be safely laundered by any process.

 Do Not Bleach: No bleach product may be used. A garment made from this yarn is not colorfast or structurally able to withstand any bleach.

 Tumble Dry, Normal: Garment made from this yarn may be dried in a machine used at the hottest available temperature setting.

 Tumble Dry, Normal, Low Heat: Garment made from this yarn may be dried in a machine regularly used at a maximum low heat setting.

 Do Not Tumble Dry: Garment made from this yarn should not be dried in a machine dryer.

 Dry Flat: Garment made from this yarn should be laid out horizontally for drying.

 Iron, Low: Garment made from this yarn can be ironed, either steam or dry, but may be done at Low setting (110° centigrade, 230° Fahrenheit).

Symbol	Meaning

 Do Not Iron: Garment made from this yarn may not be smoothed or finished with an iron.

 Dry Clean, Any Solvent: Garment made from this yarn may be dry cleaned in any solvent.

 Dry Clean Petroleum Solvent Only: Garment made from this yarn may be dry cleaned in a petroleum solvent only.

 Do Not Dry Clean: Garment made from this yarn may not be commercially dry cleaned.

Note: Even if the label says that the yarn is washable, either by machine or by hand, it's a good idea to test the yarn before you complete an entire project that may require frequent washing. You might want to try using the gauge swatch that you make according to the instructions on page 39.

The Importance of Gauge

Many new crocheters tend to shy away from gauge as if it were a dirty word. Gauge, however, is the most important word in the crocheter's dictionary. It is the most important lesson a crocheter can learn!

As a crocheter, if you want the garments that you will make to fit properly; if you want the afghans to be the correct size; and if you want to be sure that you have enough yarn to complete a project, then you need to follow the gauge given in a pattern.

Gauge simply means the number of stitches per inch, and the number of rows per inch that result from a specified yarn worked with a crochet hook in a specified size. However, since everyone crochets differently—some loosely, some tightly, some in between—the measurements of individual work can vary greatly, even when the crocheters use the same size hook and the same size yarn.

The hook sizes given in instructions are only guides. You should never go ahead with a project without making a 4" square to check your gauge. The crocheter has the responsibility to make sure to achieve the gauge specified in the pattern. You may need to use a different size hook from that specified in the pattern. Those hook sizes given in instructions are just guides, and they should never be used without first making a gauge swatch.

Here's how you make a swatch to check your gauge. At the beginning of every crochet pattern, you'll find a gauge given such as the one below. The pattern has called for a size J/10 (6mm) crochet hook.

Gauge
12 stitches = 4" in single crochet
14 rows = 4"

This actually means that you will work your gauge swatch in single crochet stitch and will try to achieve a gauge of 3 stitches and 3.5 rows to an inch. You must make a gauge swatch of at least 4" square to adequately test your work. Chain 13 and work in single crochet stitch with 12 single crochet stitches in each row for 14 rows. Finish off.

Place the swatch on a flat surface and pin it out. Be careful not to stretch the crocheting. Measure the outside edges; the sample should be a 4" square.

Now measure the center 2" and count the actual stitches and rows per inch.

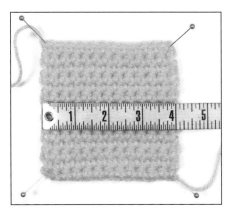 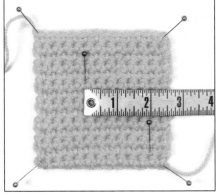

If you have more stitches or rows per inch than listed in the pattern, make another gauge swatch with a size larger hook. If you have fewer stitches or rows per inch than specified, make another swatch with a size smaller hook.

Sometimes you may find that you have the correct stitch gauge, but you are unable to get the row gauge, even with another hook. If so, don't be concerned; the stitch gauge is more important than the row gauge, and if you get the stitch gauge to work, your crocheting will work. The only place where an incorrect row gauge might be a problem is in crocheting raglan sweaters where both gauges must be perfect.

Once you have begun a pattern, it's not a bad idea to check your gauge every few inches. Sometimes if you become very relaxed, your crocheting can become looser; if you become tense, your crocheting can become tighter. To keep your gauge, you might need to change hooks in the middle of a project.

Making gauge swatches before starting a project takes time, and it is a bother. But if you miss this important step, you'll never be able to create beautiful projects that fit.

Reading a Pattern

Crochet patterns are actually written in a special language which consists of abbreviations, symbols, asterisks, parentheses, colons, daggers and brackets. This special "shorthand" is used so that instructions don't take up too much space. In the beginning they may seem confusing, but once you learn them, you will have no trouble in following them.

Skill Levels

Before beginning a project, it is a good idea to find out the skill level of a pattern. Here are the standard skill level icons developed by the Craft Yarn Council. Each of these icons, which appear with crochet patterns in books, magazines, leaflets, on yarn labels or on web sites, is a horizontal bar divided into four sections. When one section of the bar is shaded, it indicates a beginner pattern; four shaded sections indicate a pattern for experienced crocheters.

BEGINNER

Beginner: Projects for first-time crocheters using basic stitches. Minimal shaping.

EASY

Easy: Projects using yarn with basic stitches, repetitive stitch patterns, simple color changes, and simple shaping and finishing.

INTERMEDIATE

Intermediate: Projects using a variety of techniques, such as basic lace patterns or color patterns, mid-level shaping and finishing.

EXPERIENCED

Experienced: Projects with intricate stitch patterns, techniques and dimension, such as non-repeating patterns, multi-color techniques, fine threads, small hooks, detailed shaping and refined finishing.

Standard Abbreviations

approx	approximately
beg	beginning
bet	between
bl	back loop(s)
BP	back post
BPdc	back post double crochet
BPsc	back post single crochet
BPtr	back post triple crochet
ch(s)	chain(s)
ch sp(s)	chain space(s)
cm	centimeter
cont	continue
dc	double crochet
dc2tog	double crochet 2 stitches together: decrease made
dc dec	double crochet decrease
dc inc	double crochet increase
dec	decrease
dtr	double triple crochet
fig	figure
fl	front loop
foll	following
FP	front post
FPdc	front post double crochet
FPsc	front post single crochet
FPtr	front post triple crochet
g	grams
hdc	half double crochet

hdc2tog	half double crochet 2 stitches together: decrease made
hdc dec	half double crochet decrease
inc	increase(ing)
lp(s)	loop(s)
mm	millimeter
oz	ounce(s)
patt	pattern
prev	previous
rem	remain(ing)
rep	repeat(ing)
rev sc	reverse single crochet
rnd(s)	round(s)
RS	right side
sc	single crochet
sc2tog	single crochet 2 stitches together: decrease made
sc dec	single crochet decrease
sk	skip
sl	slip
sl st	slip stitch
sp(s)	space(s)
st(s)	stitch(es)
tch	turning chain
tog	together
tr	triple (or treble) crochet
tr2tog	triple crochet 2 stitches together: decrease made
WS	wrong side
yd(s)	yard(s)
YO	yarn over hook

Standard Symbols

   * An asterisk (or double asterisks**) in a pattern row indicates a portion of instructions to be used more than once. For instance, "rep from * three times" means that after working the instructions once, you must work them again three times for a total of 4 times in all.

   † A dagger (or double daggers ††) indicates that those instructions will be repeated again later in the same row or round.

   : The number of stitches after a colon tells you the number of stitches you will have when you have completed the row or round.

   ( ) Parentheses enclose instructions which are to be worked the number of times following the parentheses. For instance, "(sc, ch 1, sc) 3 times" means that you will work one single crochet, chain one, and then work one single crochet again, three times for a total of six single crochets and three chains. Parentheses often set off or clarify a group of stitches to be worked into the same space or stitch. For instance, "(dc, ch 2, dc) in corner space."

[ ] Brackets and ( ) parentheses are also used to give you additional information. For instance, "(rem sts are left unworked)."

Standard Terms

Finish off: This means to end your piece by cutting your yarn several inches beyond the last stitch worked and pulling the yarn end through the last loop remaining on the hook. This will prevent the work from unraveling.

Continue in Pattern (Patt) as Established: This means to follow the pattern stitch as it has been set up, working any increases or decreases in such a way that the pattern remains the same as it was established.

Work even: This means that the work is continued in the pattern as established without increasing or decreasing.

Right Side: This means the side of the garment that will be seen.

Wrong Side: This means the side of the garment that is inside when the garment is worn.

Right Front: This means the part of the garment that will be worn on the right side of the body.

Left Front: This means the part of the garment that will be worn on the left side of the body.

Working a Pattern

If you'd like to try your hand at reading and working a pattern, here are patterns as they would appear in a book, a magazine or online (except we've added breaks and spacing for clarity). To help you, we've given you a "translation" of several lines to explain what is happening. It's almost as if you had a crocheting friend sitting with you as you work.

If you've never worked a published pattern before, you might want to start with the easier ones–the Fabulous Facecloth or the Delightful Dishcloth–before attempting the Scarf on page 60.

FABULOUS FACECLOTH

Pattern

 **BEGINNER**

Translation

See the definition of "Beginner" on page 42.

Size

10" wide x 10" high

Materials

Worsted weight cotton **MEDIUM 4**
   yarn [100% cotton, 2.5 oz,
   120 yards (70.9 grams,
   109 meters) per ball]
   1 ball pink

Note: Photographed model
   made with Lily Sugar 'n
   Cream® #1740 Hot Pink

Size H (5 mm) crochet hook
   (or size required for gauge)

Yarn needle

Here is information about the yarn that was used to make the photographed model. The chart on page 96 will explain more about number 4 yarn. This line tells you how many ounces or yards come on each ball or skein of the chosen yarn brand so that you can determine how much yarn you would need if you choose another number 4 yarn. It also tells you the fiber content of the yarn that was used.

Gauge

14 sc = 4"

15 rows = 4"

Often instructions for a special pattern are given. Here, the pattern is single crochet for the stitch gauge (the width) and is 15 rows for the row gauge (the height). For your gauge swatch, you should have 14 single crochet stitches measuring 4" wide and 15 rows measuring 4" high.

Stitch Guide

Single crochet decrease (sc dec): Insert hook in first specified st and draw up a lp, insert hook in 2nd specified st and draw up a lp, YO and draw through all 3 lps on hook: sc dec made.

The Stitch Guide will tell you how to work special stitches that are not your normal single crochet, double crochet, etc. In this case, you are told how to work a single crochet decrease, which is worked into 2 stitches as described in this section of the pattern.

Instructions

Ch 34 loosely.

Chain 34 stitches. To do this, make a slip knot and then chain 34 stitches "loosely" so that the stitches are loose enough to be worked into. If you need help chaining, see pages 74-76.

Row 1 (right side): Sc in 2nd ch from hook and in each rem ch across: 33 sc; ch 1, turn.

This tells you that this row is the right side and means: Single crochet in the second chain from the hook and in each remaining chain across. You should have 33 single crochet stitches at the end of the row. Chain 1 and turn your work at the end of the row. If you need help in working a single crochet, see pages 77-79.

Row 2: Sc in first sc; *ch 1, skip next sc, sc in next sc; repeat from * across: 17 sc and 16 ch-1 sps; ch 1, turn.

Row 2 begins with working a single crochet in the first single crochet. Now work the stitches after the asterisk (*) across the row: chain 1 stitch, skip the next single crochet, and single crochet in the next single crochet. At the end of the row, you should have 17 single crochet and 16 chain-1 spaces. Chain 1 and turn at the end of this row.

Row 3: Sc in first sc, sc in next ch-1 sp; *ch 1, skip next sc, sc in next ch-1 sp; repeat from * across to last sc; sc in last sc: 18 sc and 15 ch-1 sps; ch 1, turn.

Row 3 begins with working a single crochet in the first single crochet. Then work a single crochet in the next chain-1 space. Now work the stitches after the asterisk (*) across the row until one single crochet remains: chain 1, skip the next single crochet and single crochet in the next chain-1 space. Then single crochet in the last single crochet. You should have 18 single crochet and 15 chain-1 spaces at the end of this row. Chain 1 and turn your work at the end of the row.

Row 4: Sc in first sc; *ch 1, skip next sc, sc in next ch-1 sp; repeat from * across to last 2 sc; ch 1, skip next sc, sc in last sc: 17 sc and 16 ch-1 sps; ch 1, turn.

Row 4 begins with working a single crochet in the first single crochet. Now work the stitches after the asterisk (*) across the row until you reach the last 2 single crochet: chain 1, skip the next single crochet and single crochet in the next chain-1 space. Then chain 1, skip the next single crochet and single crochet in the last single crochet. You should have 17 single crochet and 16 chain-1 spaces at the end of this row. Chain 1 and turn at the end of the row.

Rows 5 through 34: Repeat Rows 3 and 4, 15 times.

Repeat these 2 rows (Rows 3 and 4, alternately) 15 times for a total of 34 rows worked.

Row 35: Sc in each sc and ch-1 sp across: 33 sc; ch 1, do not turn.

Row 35 is worked with 1 single crochet in each of the single crochets and chain-1 spaces. You should have 33 single crochet at the end of this row. Chain 1 at the end of the row, but do not turn your work.

Edging

Working across side edge and starting with Row 34, *sc in edge of next 5 rows, sc dec in edge of next 2 rows, (sc in edge of next 9 rows, sc dec in edge of next 2 rows) 2 times, sc in edge of next 5 rows*;...

Now work an edging around the entire facecloth. To begin, work along the left side edge by skipping the edge of Row 35 and working 1 single crochet in the edge of each of the next 5 rows (Rows 34-30). Work 1 single crochet decrease in the edge of the next 2 rows (Rows 29 and 28). Now work the stitches in the parentheses two times. Then work 1 single crochet in the edge of each of the next 5 rows.

...working in free lps of foundation chs along bottom edge, 3 sc in first ch, sc in each ch across to last ch, 3 sc in last ch;...

Now work into the free loop of each foundation chain along the bottom edge. Work 3 sc in the first foundation chain, 1 single crochet in each of the next 31 foundation chains, and 3 single crochet in the last foundation chain.

...starting with Row 1, repeat from * to * across other side edge, skip edge of Row 35;...

Next, work your stitches along the other side edge of the rows in the same manner as on the left-hand side edge, working the same instructions between the asterisks (starting with Row 1, ending with Row 34 and skipping the edge of Row 35).

...working across Row 35, 3 sc in first sc, sc in each sc across to last sc, 3 sc in last sc: 136 sc; join with sl st in first sc.

Now work across the last row. Begin by working 3 single crochet in the first single crochet, 1 single crochet in each of the next 31 single crochet, and 3 single crochet in the last single crochet. End by joining with a slip stitch in the first single crochet. You should have a total of 136 single crochet in the edging.

Finish off; weave in ends.

Finish off and weave in ends. If you need help, see pages 94 and 95.

DELIGHTFUL DISHCLOTH

Pattern

■■□□D **EASY**

Size

About 9¹/₂" wide x 10" high

Materials

Worsted weight cotton  yarn [100% cotton, 2.5 oz, 120 yards (70.9 grams, 109 meters) per ball]
1 ball blue

Note: Photographed model made with Lily Sugar 'n Cream #1742 Hot Blue

Size H (5 mm) crochet hook (or size required for gauge)

Yarn needle

Translation

See the definition of "Easy" on page 42.

Here is information about the yarn that was used to make the photographed model. The chart on page 96 will explain more about number 4 yarn. This line tells you how many ounces or yards come on each ball or skein of the chosen yarn brand so that you can determine how much yarn you would need if you choose another number 4 yarn. It also tells you the fiber content of the yarn that was used.

Gauge

13 sc = 4"

Rows 1 through 9 = 4"

Often instructions for a special pattern are given. Here, the pattern is single crochet stitches for the stitch gauge (the width), as well as the first 9 rows of the pattern for the row gauge (height). For your gauge swatch, you should have 13 single crochet stitches measuring 4" wide. You should also have the first 9 rows of the pattern (a total of 5 rows of single crochet and 4 rows of double crochet) measuring 4" high.

Instructions

Ch 30.

Chain 30 stitches. To do this, make a slip knot and then chain 30 stitches loosely so that the stitches are loose enough to be worked into. If you need help chaining, see pages 74-76.

Row 1 (right side): Sc in 2nd ch from hook and in each rem ch across: 29 sc; ch 3 (counts as first dc of next row), turn.

This tells you that this row is the right side and means: Single crochet in the second chain from the hook and in each remaining chain across. You should have 29 single crochet stitches at the end of the row. Chain 3 and turn your work at the end of the row. The chain 3 will count as the first double crochet on Row 2. If you need help in working a single crochet, see pages 77-79.

Row 2: Skip first sc, dc in next sc; *ch 1, skip next sc, dc in next 2 sc; repeat from * across: 20 dc and 9 ch-1 sps; ch 1, turn.

Row 2 begins with skipping the first single crochet, then working a double crochet in the next single crochet. Work the stitches after the asterisk (*) across the row: chain 1 stitch, skip the next single crochet and work 1 double crochet in each of the next 2 single crochet. At the end of the row, you should have 20 double crochet and 9 chain-1 spaces. Chain 1 and turn at the end of this row. If you need help in working a double crochet, see pages 81-83.

Row 3: Sc in each dc and ch-1 sp across: 29 sc; ch 3 (counts as first dc of next row), turn.

Row 3 is comprised of working a single crochet in each of the double crochet and a single crochet in each of the chain-1 spaces. At the end of this row, work the last single crochet in the third chain of the turning chain-3 at the end of Row 1. You should have 29 single crochet at the end of this row. Chain 3 and turn your work at the end of the row.

Rows 4 through 21: Repeat Rows 2 and 3, 9 times. At end of last row, ch 1, do not turn.

Repeat these 2 rows (Rows 2 and 3, alternately) 9 more times for a total of 21 rows worked. At the end of the last row, chain 1, but do not turn your work.

Edging

Working across side edge and starting with Row 20, *work 2 sc in edge of each dc row and sc in edge of each sc row across*;...

You will proceed to work an edging around the entire dishcloth. To begin, work along the left side edge by working 1 single crochet in the 3rd chain of the turning chain-3 space of Row 20 and 1 single crochet in the turning chain-3 space. Follow this by working 1 single crochet in the edge of the single crochet on Row 19. Alternate working 2 single crochet in the edge of each double crochet row and 1 single crochet in the edge of each single crochet row until you reach the bottom left-hand corner.

...working in free lps of foundation chs along bottom edge, 3 sc in first ch, sc in each ch across to last ch, 3 sc in last ch;...

Now you will work into the free loop of each foundation chain along the bottom edge. Work 3 sc in the first foundation chain, 1 single crochet in each of the next 27 foundation chains, and 3 single crochet in the last foundation chain.

...repeat from * to * across other side edge, skip side edge of Row 21;...

Next, work your stitches along the other side edge of the rows. Work 1 single crochet in the edge of the single crochet on Row 1. Then work 1 single crochet around the post of the double crochet on the next row and single crochet in the top of the same double crochet. Alternate working 1 single crochet in the edge of each single crochet row and 2 single crochet in the edge of each double crochet row until you reach the top right-hand corner, skipping Row 21 at the top corner.

...working across Row 21, 3 sc in first sc, sc in each sc across to last sc, 3 sc in last sc: 126 sc; join with sl st in first sc.

Finish off; weave in ends.

Work across the last row. Begin by working 3 single crochet in the first single crochet, 1 single crochet in each of the next 27 single crochet, and 3 single crochet in the last single crochet. End this edging by joining with a slip stitch in the first single crochet worked on the edging. You should have a total of 126 single crochet in the edging.

Finish off and weave in ends. If you need help, see pages 94 and 95.

SCARF

Pattern

 **EASY**

Size:

6¹/₂" wide x 60" long plus fringe

Materials

Worsted weight yarn **MEDIUM 4**
   [100% acrylic, 3.5 oz,
   170 yards (100 grams,
   156 meters) per skein]
   2 skeins gold
Note: Photographed model
   made with Lion Brand®
   Vanna's Choice #130 Honey
Size J (6 mm) crochet hook (or size
   required for gauge)
Yarn needle

Translation

See the definition of "Easy" on page 42.

Here is information about the yarn that was used to make the photographed model. The chart on page 96 will explain more about number 4 yarn. This line tells you how many ounces or yards come on each ball or skein of the chosen yarn brand so that you can determine how much yarn you would need if you choose another number 4 yarn.

Gauge

13 sc = 4"

8 rows in pattern (alternating dc and sc rows) = 4"

Often instructions for a special pattern are given. Here, the pattern is single crochet stitches for the stitch gauge (the width), as well as alternating double crochet and single crochet rows for the row gauge (height). The gauge swatch should have 13 single crochet stitches measuring 4" wide and 8 rows (4 rows of single crochet and 4 rows of double crochet) measuring 4" high.

Stitch Guide

V-stitch (V-st): Work (dc, ch 1, dc) in specified st: V-st made.

The Stitch Guide will tell you how to work special stitches.

Instructions

Ch 21.

Chain 21 stitches. To do this, make a slip knot and then chain 21 stitches loosely so that the stitches are loose enough to be worked into. If you need help chaining, see pages 74-76.

Row 1 (right side): Sc in 2nd ch from hook and in each rem ch across: 20 sc; ch 3 (counts as first dc of next row), turn.

This tells you that this row is the right side and means: Single crochet in the second chain from the hook and in each remaining chain across. You should have 20 single crochet stitches at the end of the row. Chain 3 and turn your work at the end of the row. The chain 3 will count as the first double crochet on Row 2. If you need help in working a single crochet, see pages 77-79.

Row 2: Skip first 2 sc, V-st in next sc, (skip next 2 sc, V-st in next sc) 5 times,...

Row 2 begins with skipping the first 2 single crochet, then working a V-stitch in the next single crochet. After that, work the instructions in the parentheses a total of 5 times: skip the next 2 single crochet and work a V-stitch in the next single crochet.

...skip next sc, dc in last sc: 6 V-sts and 2 dc; ch 1, turn.

Skip the next single crochet and double crochet in the last single crochet. At the end of the row, you should have 6 V-stitches (each made with 2 dc and a chain between these 2 double crochet) and 2 more double crochet. Chain 1 and turn at the end of this row. If you need help in working a double crochet, see pages 81-83.

Row 3: Sc in each dc and in each ch-1 sp across, working last sc in 3rd ch of turning ch-3: 20 sc; ch 3 (counts as first dc of next row), turn.

Row 3 is comprised of working a single crochet in each of the double crochet (including each double crochet of each V-stitch) and in each of the ch-1 spaces of each V-stitch. At the end of this row, work the last single crochet in the third chain of the turning chain-3. You should have 20 single crochet at the end of this row. Chain 3 and turn your work at the end of the row.

Repeat Rows 2 and 3, alternately until scarf is 60" long, or to desired length. At end of last row, do not ch 3 and do not turn.

Repeat these 2 rows until the scarf measures 60" long from the beginning, or to the desired length that you would like for your scarf. End by working a repeat of Row 3. At the end of the last row, do not chain 3 and do not turn your work.

Edging

Work 2 more sc in same ch as last sc worked on last row; working along edge of rows, sc in turning ch-sp, sc in edge of sc; *sc in 3rd ch of turning ch, sc in turning ch-sp, sc in edge of sc; rep from * across edge;...

You will proceed to work an edging around the entire scarf. To begin, work 2 more single crochet in the same chain where the last single crochet was worked on the last row. Then, working along the side edge of the rows, single crochet in the turning chain-3 space of the double crochet row (the row before the last row worked) and single crochet in the edge of the single crochet on the single crochet row. Then work the stitches after the asterisk (*) across the side edge until you reach the bottom edge: single crochet in the third chain of the turning chain-3 on the next double crochet row, single crochet in the turning chain-3 space itself and single crochet in the edge of the single crochet on the next single crochet row.

...working in free lps of foundation chs, 2 sc in first ch, sc in each ch across to last ch. 2 sc in last ch;...

Now work your stitches in the free loops of the foundation chains. To start, work 2 single crochet in the first chain, then single crochet in each of the remaining chains across to the last chain. Work 2 single crochet in the last chain.

...working along other edge of rows, sc in edge of sc; **sc around post of dc, sc in top of same dc, sc in edge of sc; rep from ** across edge;...

Work along the other side edge of the rows with a single crochet in the edge of the single crochet on Row 1. Then work the stitches after the double asterisks (**) across the side edge until you reach the top edge: single crochet around the post (the vertical part of the stitch below the top of the stitch) of the double crochet on the next row, single crochet in the top of the same double crochet and single crochet in the edge of the single crochet on the next row.

...working across last row, 3 sc in first sc, sc in next 19 sc; join with sl st in next sc. Finish off; weave in ends.

Begin working across the top with 3 single crochet in the first single crochet and one single crochet in each of the next 19 single crochet across to the beginning of the edging. End this edging by joining with a slip stitch in the next (first) single crochet.

Fringe

Cut 80 strands of yarn, each 12" long. Using 2 strands of yarn each, attach 20 fringes at each short end of scarf, following Fringe Instructions on pages 68 and 69. Lightly steam fringe to remove kinks in yarn. Trim fringe evenly.

This tells you how to make the fringe. Each fringe is made by holding 2 strands of yarn together. The fringes are made at both short ends of the scarf. For more information about making fringes, see pages 68 and 69.

Making Fringe and Tassels

A wonderful way to finish a
project is to add fringe or tassels.
Here are instructions for both.

Fringe

Basic Instructions

Cut a piece of cardboard about 6" wide and half as long as specified in the instructions for strands, plus $1/2$" for trimming allowance. Wind the yarn loosely and evenly lengthwise around the cardboard. When the card is filled, cut the yarn across one end. Do this several times; then begin fringing. You can wind additional strands as you need them.

Single Knot Fringe

Hold the specified number of strands for one knot of fringe together, then fold in half.

Hold the project with the right side facing you. Using a crochet hook, draw the folded ends through the space or stitch from right to wrong side.

Pull the loose ends through the folded section.

Draw the knot up firmly.

Space the knots evenly and trim the ends of the fringe.

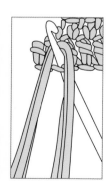 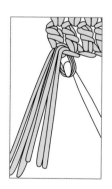 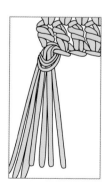 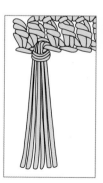

Double Knot Fringe

Begin by working Single Knot Fringe. With right side facing you and working from left to right, take half the strands of one knot and half the strands in the knot next to it, and knot them together.

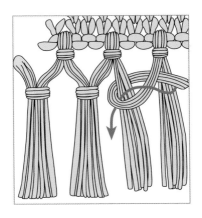

Triple Knot Fringe

First work Double Knot Fringe. Then working again on right side from left to right, tie the third row of knots, taking half the strands of one knot and half the strands in the knot next to it, and knot them together.

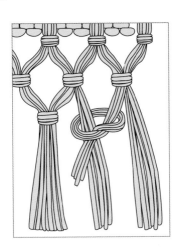

Tassels

Decide how long the desired tassel is going to be, and cut a piece of cardboard to use as a guide that is $1/2$" longer than desired length.

For tie, place a 12" piece of yarn across top of the guide. Wind the yarn around the guide and over the tie. Keep winding until the tassel is the desired thickness.

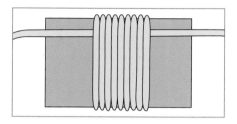

Draw the tie up tightly and knot it. Slide the yarn off the guide and cut the yarn at the bottom.

Cut another 12" yarn strip and wrap it tightly about an inch below the top of the tassel. Wrap several times and tie a secure knot. Trim the ends of the strip and the bottom of the tassel.

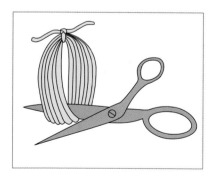

Refresher Course in Crochet

Getting Started

Before beginning to crochet, be certain that you are familiar with the crochet hook as described on page 6.

There are several ways of holding your hook and your yarn. Despite what some "experts" might tell you, there is really no right or wrong way. The way that works for you is the way you should use.

Most crocheters hold their hook in their right hand if they are right-handed or in their left hand if they are left-handed. There are two ways to hold the hook, and you should use the way that is most comfortable for you.

In the Knife Hold, you hold the crochet hook as you would hold a knife when cutting food.

In the Pencil Hold, you hold the crochet hook as you would hold a pencil.

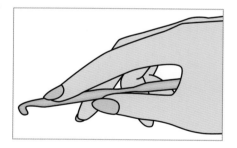 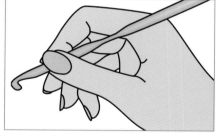

Slip Knot

A crochet pattern can be worked in rows (that is back and forth to make a flat piece such as an afghan) or in rounds (worked around to form a flat circle or a tube with no seams, such as a hat). No matter which way a pattern is worked, the first thing you need to do is to make a slip knot on the hook. Be aware that usually the pattern will assume that you know that and will not tell you to do it.

Step 1: Place the end of the yarn on a flat surface and leaving a 6" end make a loop.

Step 2: Insert the hook, pull on the end marked A and draw up a loop onto the hook.

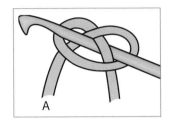

Step 3: Make certain that the knot is snug on the hook, but not too tight, so that it can slide easily. Leave the loose yarn end at least 6" long to use later.

Note: It is important to remember that the slip knot is never counted as a stitch. It is only used to start a new piece or to join new yarn.

Chain

In crochet, the chain is the foundation upon which all crochet is built. It can be confusing because the word "chain" refers to a single stitch and to the group of stitches as well.

Step 1: Holding the yarn in the dominant hand and the yarn in the other, make a slip knot on the hook.

Step 2: Take the yarn from back to front over the top of the hook, catch it with the head of the hook and draw through the slip knot on the hook and up onto the working area of the hook.

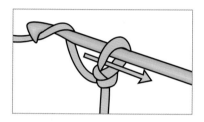

Always take the yarn over the hook from back to front, never from front to back.

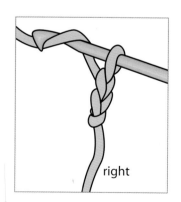

Step 3: Again take the yarn from the back to the front over the hook, catch it and draw through the loop on the hook (which is actually the first chain made). Continue making chain stitches loosely because you will be working into them. Be sure to work each stitch only on the working area of the hook

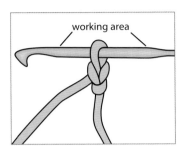

A group of chain stitches is called a "starting chain" or a "foundation chain." To make most crochet stitches, you need to make a starting chain and then work the stitches into it.

When you work a starting chain, keep moving your fingers up closer to the hook after each stitch or two to help maintain control.

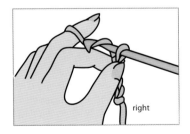
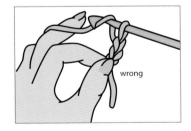

In counting stitches in crochet, never count the slip knot or the stitch on the hook.

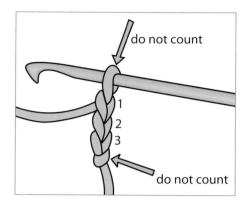

A completed starting chain will look like this. The front will look like a series of interlocked Vs, each V representing one chain stitch. On the back you will see a row of bumps. Each bump also represents one chain stitch because each V has a corresponding bump.

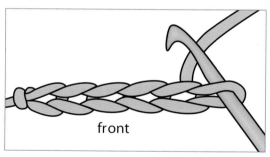

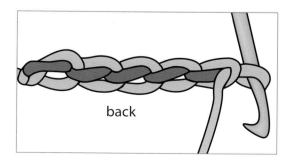

Single Crochet

Abbreviation: sc

Right Side

Step 1: Hold the chain with V side facing you, and row of chains to the left. Skip the first chain stitch from the hook and insert hook from top to bottom in the back bump of next chain stitch.

Step 2: Hook the yarn and draw it through to the front and up on to the working area of the hook.

There are now 2 loops on the hook.

Step 3: Take the yarn over the hook again from back to front (this is a "yarn over"), hook it and draw through both loops on the hook. One loop remains on the hook, and you have made one single crochet (sc) stitch.

To make other stitches, insert the hook from top to bottom in the back bump of the next chain stitch and repeat Steps 2 and 3. As you work across a starting chain, your work will look like this.

Work into the last chain stitch but not into the slip knot. One loop will remain on the hook. The loop on the hook is never counted as a stitch. Remember that you never work into the slip knot.

Wrong Side

To work another row of single crochet (sc) stitches, you have to turn the piece and work back into the sc stitches just made. Whenever a new row is begun, one or more chain stitches must be worked to bring the yarn up to the height of the next row. This is called the turning chain. When you are working with single crochet, you will need to work only one chain. Make one chain and turn the work counter clockwise.

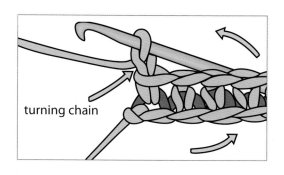

turning chain

You never work into the turning chain, unless you are specifically instructed to do so. Skip the turning chain and work one single crochet (sc) in the sc nearest your hook (which in this diagram is the last sc worked on the first row).

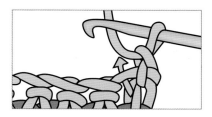

Since you are now working into a stitch, not a chain, insert the hook under the top two loops of the stitch.

Step 1: Hook the yarn and draw it through to the front and up on to the working area of the hook. There are now 2 loops on the hook.

Step 2: Take the yarn over the hook again from back to front, hook it and draw through both loops on the hook. One loop remains on the hook, and you have made one single crochet (sc) stitch.

Half Double Crochet
Abbrevation: hdc

This is a versatile crochet stitch that is slightly taller than single crochet and slightly shorter than double crochet. To work half double crochet, make the desired number of chains.

Right Side

Step 1: Yarn over the hook; insert the hook into the back bump of the third chain from the hook, yarn over and draw up a loop: there are now 3 loops on the hook.

Step 2: Yarn over again and draw the yarn through all 3 loops on the hook at one time: one hdc stitch is completed.

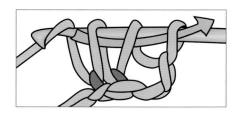

Repeat Steps 1 and 2 in each chain across the row, but in Step 1 insert the hook in the next chain instead of the 3rd chain from the hook.

At the end of the row, you will have one fewer stitch than the starting chain, counting the first 2 chains you skipped at the beginning of the row as one stitch. Ch 1 and turn the work counter-clockwise. In some patterns, a ch 2 is used to turn. If so, the ch 2 is usually counted as the first stitch of the next row. The pattern will tell you if this is done.

Wrong Side

Repeat Steps 1 and 2, working in stitches not chains, in each stitch across, ch 1 and turn.

Double Crochet

Abbreviation: dc

Dc stitches are taller than both single crochet and half double crochet stitches. Crochet stitches are made taller by adding yarn overs. To practice double crochet, make a slip knot and a row of chain stitches.

Right Side

Step 1: Bring yarn over the hook from back to front. Skip the first three chains and insert the hook into the back bump of the fourth chain from the hook.

Step 2: Hook the yarn and draw it through the fourth chain and up onto the working area of the hook. There are now 3 loops on the hook.

Step 3: Hook the yarn again and draw it though the first 2 loops on the hook. There are now 2 loops on the hook.

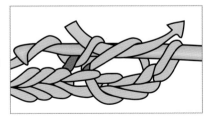

Step 4: Hook the yarn again and draw it through both of the remaining loops on the hook.

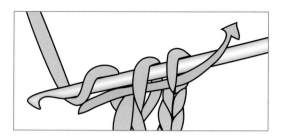

You have now made one double crochet (dc) stitch. To work the next dc stitch, repeat Step 1, but insert the hook into the back bump of the next chain rather than the fourth chain from the hook. Repeat Steps 2 through 4 again. Continue working in this manner, always working Step 1 into the next chain.

To work the next row, you will need to work a turning chain and turn the work. Because the double crochet stitches are taller than single crochet stitches and half double crochet stitches, you will need to make 3 chains to bring the yarn up to the correct height.

Then turn the work counter-clockwise.

Wrong Side

The turning chain counts as the first dc of the new row. Work your next dc in the 2nd stitch of the previous row, rather than the first stitch. It is very important to place this stitch correctly. Here are the wrong and right placements for this stitch.

Now you will be working dc stitches into the stitches of the previous row.

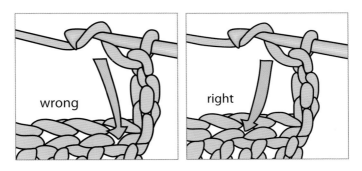

Step 1: Yarn over, insert hook under the top 2 loops (the V) of the next stitch and draw up a loop the same height as the 3 turning chains. There are now 3 loops on the hook.

Step 2: Yarn over and draw the yarn through the first 2 loops on the hook. There are now 2 loops on the hook.

Step 3: Yarn over and draw the yarn through the remaining 2 loops. You now completed one double crochet stitch.

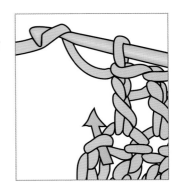

When you reach the end of the row, work the last double crochet stitch into the top chain of the turning chain of the previous row. Be careful not to miss this last stitch.

Triple Crochet Stitch

Abbreviation: tr or trc

Triple crochet, sometimes called treble crochet, is a tall stitch that works up very quickly.

Right Side

Step 1: Yarn over the hook twice, then insert the hook in the back bump of the 5th chain from the hook.

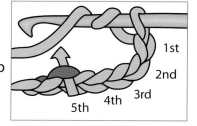

Step 2: Yarn over and draw through the chain and up to about 1" high. There are now 4 loops on the hook.

Step 3: Yarn over again and draw through the first 2 loops on the hook. There are now 3 loops on the hook.

Step 4: Yarn over and draw through the first two loops on the hook. There are now 2 loops on the hook.

Step 5: Yarn over and draw through the remaining 2 loops. One triple crochet stitch has now been completed.

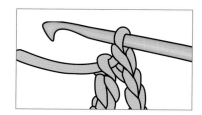

Wrong Side

Repeat Steps 1 through 5 in each stitch across; ch 4 and turn for the next row. Remember that the turning chain counts as the first stitch of the new row. Therefore, skip the first stitch and place the next triple crochet in the 2nd stitch. Work the last stitch of each row in the top of the turning chain.

Slip Stitch

Abbreviation: sl st

This stitch is used in four ways:

- To move yarn across an area without adding additional height
- To join work at the end of a piece worked in rounds instead of rows
- To join new yarn
- To join seams

Step 1: Insert hook in specified stitch, chain or loop.

Step 2: YO and draw hook through both the stitch, chain or loop and the loop on hook in one motion.

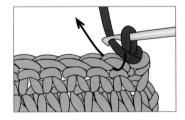

Reverse Single Crochet

This is a stitch that makes an attractive corded edging. Because it is worked in the opposite (reverse) direction from normal crochet, it is sometimes difficult to learn.

Start at the end of the row. Instead of turning to work the next row, work one chain, and then insert the hook into the next stitch to the right (or left if you are left-handed).

Now work a single crochet in the usual way.

Post Stitches

A post stitch is a stitch that is worked around the vertical bar—or post—of a stitch rather than in the top of the stitch. While they are usually worked in double crochet, they can be worked in other stitches as well. The Front Post Stitch is usually worked on the right side of a piece while the Back Post Stitch is usually worked on the wrong side of a piece.

Front Post Double Crochet Stitch

Yarn over the hook, insert the hook from the front to the back to the front again around the post of the specified stitch. Then complete the stitch as usual.

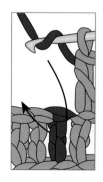

Back Post Double Crochet Stitch

Yarn over the hook, insert the hook from the back to the front to the back again around the post of the specified stitch. Then complete the stitch as usual.

Turning Chains

When you turn the work at the end of a row, a number of chains must be worked to raise the yarn to the proper height to work the stitches of the next row. Unless something else is specified in the instructions, use the following:

For sc: 1 turning chain; it does not count as a stitch on the following row so the next stitch is worked into the very first stitch of the following row.

For hdc: 2 turning chains; the chains count as the first stitch of the following row, so the first stitch is skipped and the next hdc is worked in the second stitch.

For dc: 3 turning chains; the chains count as the first stitch of the following row. The first stitch is therefore skipped and the next dc is worked in the second stitch.

For tr: 4 turning chains; the chains count as the first stitch of the following row, so the first stitch is skipped and the next tr is worked in the second stitch.

Working into the Starting Chains

For sc: Work in the 2nd ch from the hook. The skipped chains do not count as a stitch. Make one more chain than the final number of stitches needed.

For hdc: Work in the 3rd chain from the hook. The skipped chains count as a stitch. Make one more chain than the final number of stitches needed.

For dc: Work in the 4th chain from the hook. The skipped chains count as a stitch. Make two more chains than the final number of stitches needed.

For tr: Work in the 5th chain from the hook. The skipped chains count as a stitch. Make three more chains than the final number of stitches needed.

Crocheting Circles

Many crochet patterns start with a circle. The instructions will tell you to work a certain number of chains and to join them with a slip stitch (sl st) in first chain to form a ring.

Then the instructions will tell you how many stitches to work into the ring.

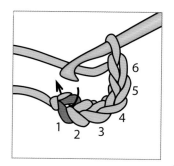 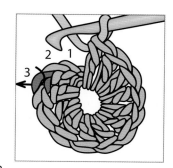

Decreasing

Usually when you are working on a project, the instructions will explain how to do the decrease. Here, however, are basic instructions for working decreases for the basic crochet stitches given here.

Single Crochet Decrease (sc2tog)

(Insert the hook in the next stitch and draw up a loop) twice. There are three loops now on the hook. Yarn over and draw through all three loops on the hook.

Single crochet decrease completed.

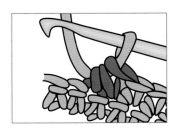

Half Double Crochet Decrease (hdc2tog)

Step 1: Yarn over, insert the hook in the next stitch and draw up a loop. There are now three loops on the hook.

Step 2: Keeping the three loops on the hook, yarn over and draw up a loop in the next stitch. There are now five loops on the hook. Hook the yarn and draw through all five loops.

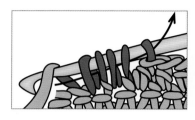

Half double crochet decrease completed.

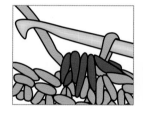

Double Crochet Decrease (dc2tog)

Step 1: Yarn over, insert hook in next stitch and draw up a loop, yarn over and draw through first two loops on hook. Two loops remain on the hook.

Step 2: Keeping two loops on the hook, work another dc in the next stitch until three loops remain on the hook. Yarn over and draw through all three loops.

Double crochet decrease completed.

Triple Crochet Decrease (tr2tog)

Step 1: Yarn over twice. Insert the hook in the next stitch and draw up a loop. (Yarn over and draw though first two loops on the hook) twice. Two loops remain on the hook.

Step 2: Keeping these 2 loops on the hook, work another triple crochet in the next st until three loops remain on the hook. Yarn over and draw through all three loops.

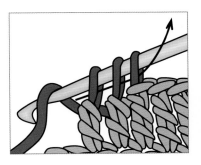

Triple crochet decrease completed.

Increases

Increases in single, double, half double and triple crochet are made by working two or more stitches in the same stitch. Increases in complicated stitches are usually given with the pattern instructions.

Single crochet increase

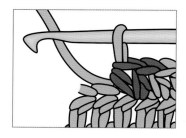

Half double crochet increase

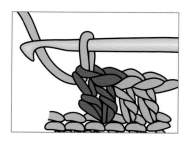

Double crochet increase

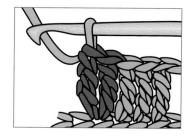

Triple crochet increase

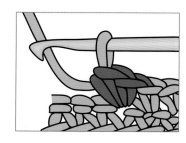

Joining Yarn

When joining a new ball of yarn, try to make it at the end of a row whenever possible. Make certain that you will have enough yarn to complete a row before you start it. Work the last stitch in the row until one final step remains. Then drop the old yarn to the back, leaving the loop on the hook. Cut the old yarn off, leaving a 6" yarn end for weaving in later. Hold the new yarn behind the work and complete the last step of the stitch with the new yarn.

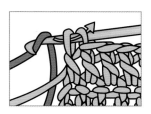

Make the turning chain with the new yarn and continue with it. If you need to change colors in the middle of a row, use the same technique, working the last step of the final stitch of the old color with the new color. Cut the old color and continue with the new color.

Finishing Off

When you have finished a crochet piece, cut the yarn several inches beyond the last stitch worked, leaving a 6" end. Draw the end through the last loop remaining on the hook. This will prevent the work from unraveling.

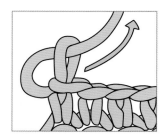

Seaming

Usually the pattern that you are following will give you instructions on joining pieces together. Use the same yarn you used in the project unless the yarn is too thick. In that case, untwist the yarn (if possible) and use fewer plies, or use a thinner yarn in the same color.

If you have no instructions, here is a simple overcast seam that can be used for many projects. It not only makes a fairly flat seam, but it is easy to do.

Step 1: Hold two pieces with right sides together. Stitching will take place on the wrong side.

Step 2: Thread an 18" length of yarn into a yarn needle. Anchor the yarn by running it through the backs of the stitches for a few inches.

Step 3: Bring the needle from the back through the top two loops of the first stitch of the bottom piece then through the top two loops of the front piece. Pull the yarn all the way through. Make the stitch snug but not too tight.

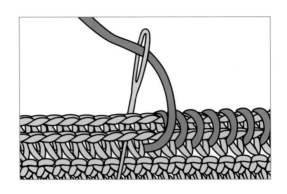

Step 4: Take the yarn over the work and to the back again. Bring the needle through the top two loops of both stitches again. Draw the yarn up tightly and take over the work and to the back again.

Step 5: At end, cut yarn and weave in yarn end.

Weaving in the Ends

When you have completed all of your crocheting, you may find yarn ends just hanging there loosely. Thread the ends in a yarn needle. Working on the wrong side of your crocheting, weave the needle in and out of the backs of several of your stitches. Then weave again in another direction. Weave about 2" in one direction and 1" in the opposite direction. Trim off any extra yarn.

Never permit your yarn needle to go through to the front of the project.

Index

Abbreviations, 43, 44
Ball band, 30-34
Chain, 74, 75, 76
Decreasing, 89, 90, 91
Double crochet, 81-83, 86,
 87, 88, 90, 91, 92
Fibers, 25-29
Finish off, 46, 94
Foundation chain, 75, 76
Gauge swatch, 38-40
Half double crochet, 79, 80,
 87, 88, 90, 92
Increasing, 92
Knife hold, 72
Label, 30-34
Laundering, 33-36
Patterns, 48-66
Pencil hold, 72

Post stitches, 86, 87
Reverse single crochet, 86
Seaming, 94, 95
Single crochet, 77-79, 87,
 88, 92
Skill levels, 42
Slip knot, 72, 73
Slip stitch, 85
Starting chain, 88
Symbols, 45
Terms, 46
Thread hooks, 6, 14-15
Treble crochet, 84
Triple crochet, 84, 85, 87,
 88, 91, 92
Turning chains, 87
Yarn hooks, 6-13
Yarn label, 30-34

Standard Yarn Weights

To make it easier for yarn manufacturers, publishers, and designers to prepare consumer-friendly products and for consumers to select the right materials for a project, the following standard yarn weight system has been adopted. Categories of yarn, gauge, ranges, and recommended hook sizes.

Yarn Weight Symbol & Names	LACE 0	SUPER FINE 1	FINE 2	LIGHT 3	MEDIUM 4	BULKY 5	SUPER BULKY 6
Type of Yarns in Category	Fingering, 10-count crochet thread	Sock, Fingering Baby	Sport, Baby	DK, Light Worsted	Worsted, Afghan, Aran	Chunky, Craft, Rug	Bulky, Roving
Crochet Gauge* Ranges in Single Crochet to 4" (10 cm)	32-42 double crochets**	21-32 sts	16-20 sts	12-17 sts	11-14 sts	8-11 sts	5-9 sts
Advised Hook Size Range	Steel*** 6,7,8 Regular hook B-1	B-1 to E-4	E-4 to 7	7 to I-9	I-9 to K-10.5	K-10.5 to M-13	M-13 and larger

*GUIDELINES ONLY: The chart above reflects the most commonly used gauges and hook sizes for specific yarn categories.

** Lace weight yarns are usually crocheted on larger-size hooks to create lacy openwork patterns. Accordingly, a gauge range is difficult to determine. Always follow the gauge stated in your pattern.

*** Steel crochet hooks are sized differently from regular hooks—the higher the number the smaller the hook, which is the reverse of regular hook sizing.